Long Ago and Today

by John Serrano

People lived in towns long ago.
People worked and played
in towns.

People still live in towns today. People work and play in towns, too.

In some ways, towns long ago were like they are today.

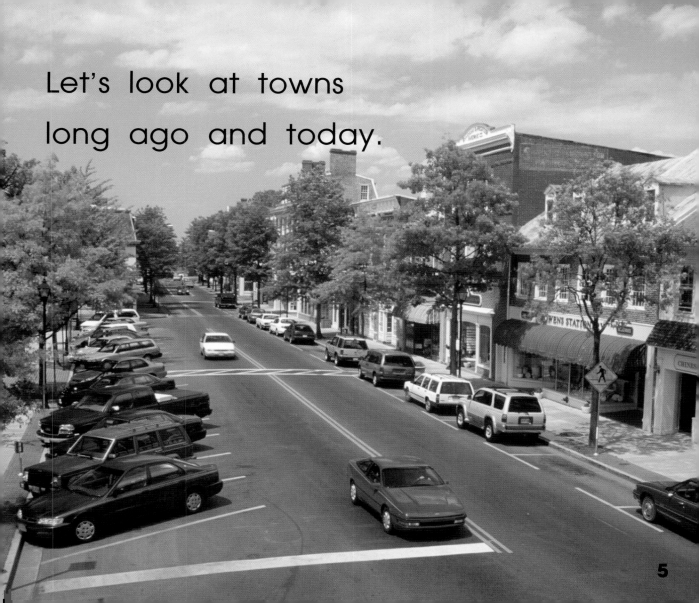

Let's look at towns
long ago and today.

This is a train station long ago.

This is a train station today.

Look at this fire station long ago.

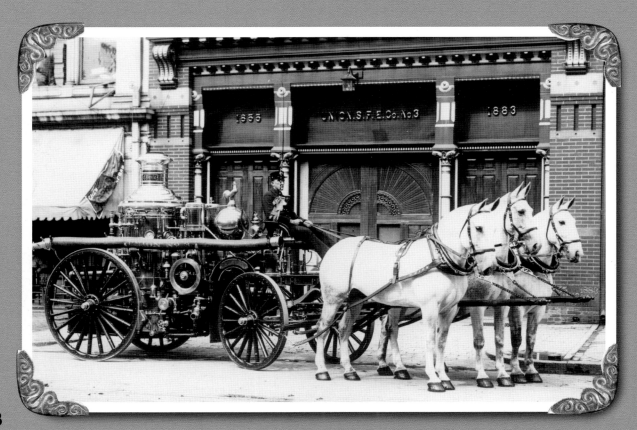

Look at this fire station today.

Some children went to
this school long ago.

Some children go to
this school today, too.

This store sold food long ago.

This store sells food today.

People played in
this park long ago.

People still play in
the same park today.

Find photos of your town long ago. How is your town the same today as it was long ago?